Blessing

THE NEXT
GENERATION

Blessing the Next Generation: Releasing God's Best in Your Child

Printed in the United States of America

ISBN-10: 0-9988226-0-4

ISBN-13: 978-0-9988226-0-0

Learn more information at: www.PatAndCandy.com

Published by: Eagle Wings Books

Publishing and Design Services: MartinPublishingServices.com

Blessing

THE NEXT
GENERATION

RELEASING GOD'S BEST
IN YOUR CHILD'S LIFE

PAT FENNER

DEDICATION

To my husband, Paul,
who has always encouraged me to
share with others the lessons I've learned in life;

and our children
Chris, Lauren, Josh, Matt and Hope,
who were and are our blessings:
the ones who inspired this celebration in our family.

To God be the glory!

Contents

Foreword

REMEMBER THE THRILL AND JOY that came to you as God ushered into your home His gift of a child? Those unforgettable moments were filled with praise and thanksgiving to the awesome God for blessing us with such a gracious gift. With these expressions of gratitude also came the sobering reminder that it was our responsibility as parents to train the child in the knowledge of Scripture and nurture a love for God. Then the day would come that the love for God would blossom into an act of faith in Christ as Savior. That child was designed by God to be a blessing to others. For all that to come to fruition, it would be the responsibility of we parents, knowing full well that our own personal abilities were not sufficient to accomplish the entrusted task, to daily trust the Lord for guidance and spiritual insight.

In our family, prayerful searching of the Scriptures revealed the wealth of divine resources to instill God's ways and thinking into our children. Thus began the journey to fulfill the admonition to train the child in the way he should go. It would involve much study and preparation on our part. Creative ways of presenting and implementing Biblical concepts and practices became topics of conversation with friends who also shared our mission. It was encouraging to know that we were not alone in these endeavors. Other Christian families shared the urgency of blessing their children and having them become a blessing to others.

The examples given in this book are being implemented in many Christian homes. Role playing, puppet characters, stories and songs, reciting Bible verses, videos, and Christian children's books all play an important part in blessing the lives of the very young. But what can be done to recognize their entrance into adulthood? In this book you will be challenged to offer a blessing service for your young adult, "being confident of this, that he who began a good work in you will carry it on to completion."

Dr. Harry Martinez

Preface

OVER FIFTEEN YEARS AGO, OUR oldest son turned 13. It was an inspiring time for us as parents, and we look back at that first blessing service as a significant moment in our family's history.

About a year prior, when Paul and I were coming to grips with having our first son enter the teenage years, we started thinking and talking and praying about what we could do to make that transition year memorable and important. We headed to Scripture, and searched it to see what ceremonies or activities we could possibly adapt from the Hebrew tradition and the early church. For years we had already been celebrating a Christian Passover as a family, so that wasn't really a far stretch for us. We also sought current or popular materials on the blessing, but were somewhat dismayed at what was available at the time. The few books we could find were dull and dry, not really engaging and a bit too, um, conceptual. Of course, God uses all things for good (Romans 8:28), so despite the dearth of information, the net result was something that truly reflected not only our family's beliefs, but also the vision and prayers we had for our son, and subsequent children. How it has evolved and been used over the years is something totally beyond what we could ever have imagined.

This book gives you some insight into the "why's" and the "how's" of a Christian Blessing service. The roots of this ceremony are intertwined with the Bar Mitzvah, a ceremony that is a part of the Hebrew roots of the Christian faith. We celebrate this event with family and friends as part of both our sons' and daughters' 13th birthdays. Much more than "just a party", our blessing service is a way to welcome them to the world of young adulthood, to remind them of the support and guidance that is available to them through loving friends and family, and to encourage them to grow into the plan God has created for them before the beginning of time (Ephesians 2:10).

It is our prayer that these words may encourage you to craft a milestone event in your own children's lives that will serve a similar purpose. Without intending to sound morose, the days are indeed growing more difficult as time passes. Indeed, God's Word warns us that it will get worse before it gets better! May you seek to strengthen and support your children while they are under your influence, in order that they may grow to stand firm in the faith, be a light and influence in their circles, and, in the end, finish the race well. (2 Timothy 4:7)

Warmly,

Pat

Introduction

IN 2010 PAT AND I had the tremendous opportunity to travel to Israel. There were countless powerful images and memories, but none stronger than what I saw at the Western Wall in Jerusalem.

This has been a site for Jewish prayer and pilgrimage for centuries and is arguably the most sacred site recognized by the Jewish faith outside of the Temple Mount itself. There were thousands of people there praying, reading from the Torah, and just visiting.

The day included several dozen families coming to the Wall to celebrate the Bar Mitzvah of their sons. Some waved banners, some carried canopies to shield from the sun. Some played stringed instruments, cymbals, and trumpets. Some called out "Make way!" so the crowd would make room for the young celebrant. Some boys walked, others were carried on the shoulders of their fathers. Each family celebrated in their own unique way, while joining in the assembly of the crowd to mark this significant event.

I noticed the joy. The boys were obviously excited (and a bit scared and embarrassed). But the fathers… I'd never seen a group of men who were prouder, or wore bigger smiles. There was no shame in announcing their boys becoming men. And as the boys approached the Torah and read from it publicly, all prayed and listened, including the oldest Rabbis.

It struck me that I had never seen such a celebration in my life. I know proud fathers, but I'd never seen one announce to a crowd of strangers how proud he was of his son, or lift his son to his shoulders and carry him through the public streets.

And I had never seen a culture corporately lift up and celebrate a rite of passage into adulthood like I was witnessing.

They marked the moment in a manner that could never be forgotten. And they would not be stopped. At one point an unattended bag became a bomb scare, and the area was evacuated. Instead of running, or cowering in fear, the families took the party to the streets. They continued to carry their sons, singing in praise and celebration.

This is not some ancient text or outdated ritual.

It happens today.

Our children need to know.

They need to know when they have arrived at adulthood.

They need to look forward to the moment in anticipation, and prepare for it with diligence.

They need to hear their fathers and mothers speak blessings into their lives, and utter the dreams they hold inside.

They need to be celebrated in a way that cannot be forgotten, and lifted up by the community with confidence and boldness.

Creating that occasion is what these pages are all about.

Paul Fenner

1

The Importance of Blessing

"Words are powerful; take them seriously."

Matthew 12: 36 (The Message)

FOR THE BELIEVER, ALL ONE has to do is take a look at the Scriptures to understand and find examples of that principle in action.

From God speaking the world into creation in Genesis to Jesus' words on the cross, announcing that salvation and forgiveness were made available to all upon His death…the Bible is rife with examples of the importance of words.

The book of Proverbs gives us many lessons and teachings about the power of our tongue, and ways to train and guard what comes out of it.

In the New Testament, people near and far were amazed at the words of Jesus Himself, and there are over 400 specific references to the word "word", from the simple and mundane to the deep and symbolic.

Just as importantly, we as parents – and specifically, dads – are our children's first exposure to the concept of God as Father. God uses the Scriptures to "teach, rebuke, correct and train" (2 Timothy 3:16) us as His children, and we have both the right and the privilege to use the Bible in the same way with the children with whom God has chosen to bless us.

The Importance Of Blessing

The first mention of a parental blessing is seen in Genesis 27, when Abraham blesses Jacob. In this particular instance, the blessing is reserved for the eldest son. Because he is getting old in years, Abraham calls Esau to his side and asks him to fix a delicious meal in preparation to receive a special blessing. Rebekah, of course, is particularly fond of their younger son, Jacob, and arranges things so that, in the end, Jacob is the recipient. It's interesting to note Esau's response. He weeps with a loud and bitter cry (v.34, 38) at the thought that there may be no blessing for him, and pleads three separate times for a blessing – *some* form of blessing - from his father (v. 34, 36, 38). Clearly, this was something highly valued and strongly desired.

Other examples of the blessing can be found in the Old Testament. In Genesis 49: 1-28, Jacob prayed for each of his 12 sons in a blessing format. Later on, Aaron prayed for the congregation in that well-known prayer found in Numbers 6:24-26.

> "*The* LORD bless you and keep you;
> *the* LORD make his face shine on you
> *and be gracious to you;*
> *the* LORD turn his face toward you,
> and give you peace.'"

In the New Testament, of course, Jesus had a heart for children, clearly seen not only in how He referred to children, but also how He intentionally blessed them (Mark 10:13-16, Matthew 19:13 and Luke 18:16).

When we gather together with others who share our heart for our child...

"For the mouth speaks what the heart is full of. A good man brings good things out of the good stored up in him..."

Matt 12: 34-35 (NIV)

... the Lord honors our prayers for them.

"Again, truly I tell you that if two of you on earth agree about anything they ask for, it will be done for them by my Father in heaven. For where two or three gather in my name, there am I with them."

Matt 18:19-20 (NIV)

Blessing

THE NEXT
GENERATION

2

Modern Milestones
vs. Spiritual Stepping Stones

BRINGING THIS INTO OUR CURRENT age, what events can you think of that signify a child's growing up?

Let's see, first boyfriend/girlfriend (although I hear parents talking that way about their *pre-schoolers*! Ugh!), maybe first date, getting their license, first drink, ears pierced (I guess this one could be for boys now, too), sweet-16 birthday, registering to vote or entering the Armed Forces...

These have become what I call modern milestones. And while they may indeed have some significance, at best they are events on a timeline. In and of themselves, they add no character to our children's lives, provide no preparation for their future, and neither strengthen nor build their faith or journey with the Lord. They are both temporal and temporary.

These modern milestones quite often occur during what we call "adolescence". This period of time is roughly considered between the ages of 13 and 19, when children undergo physiological changes and begin to transition their roles in the family, resulting in an often very emotional and stressful period of life. Interestingly enough, however, this time of life did not even exist as a particular life-period prior to the late 19th century. Additionally, it was not given serious study until the early 20th century, and is generally considered to be an American "discovery". (source)

Whatever you call it, it is during this time that our children/young adults need a steady voice to guide them. They won't ask us, they usually won't seek us out, and they may often appear to be turning a deaf ear to us, but we should not be deterred. Establishing spiritual stepping-stones are *crucial* in the spiritual life of our children, requiring a concerted effort on our part. But instituting the blessing, and a proper attitude towards blessing in our day-to-day lives, will help fulfill the often-used Proverb:

"Train up a child in the way he should go,
And when he is old he will not depart from it.

Proverbs 22:6 (NKJ)

3

A Father's Thoughts

A **BLESSING SERVICE CAN BE DONE** at any age. We do them at 13. It just feels right. But there is an important thing to keep in mind. Many people I speak with want to wait until later. They don't feel their children are ready for "adulthood". However, the truth is you don't do a blessing because they are ready. *You do a blessing to MAKE them ready*, and to make a personal commitment for which you yourself might not be ready!

To be honest, 12 or 13 is at the very least an awkward age, filled with uncomfortable challenges and growth spurts. All the hormonal stuff is happening, and there is so much change going on that things are often downright unpleasant. Honestly, I don't always enjoy my kids that much at that age. Plus, there is this monster on the horizon called "teenager", and it is beginning to rear its ugly head. These kids are children, and they are at arguably the most confused and chaotic moment of their lives. They've lost their adorable childishness, and have no confidence in their adulthood. They are just not much fun to be around.

It's at this moment in the Jewish faith that families call their children "adults". They invite them into the family business as partners, and begin to treat them as equals.

ARE THEY *NUTS*??

But I've noticed something interesting in Scripture. There is no mention of the word or concept of a "teenager". There are adults, and there are children. And there is no presumed never-never land of lost foolishness in between where we throw away our progeny and accept that they are going to act like idiots for a few years. They are either children, or adults.

This observation was kind of uncomfortable to me. I liked my kids. I liked being a parent. I don't really like change. But then I realized that the desire of my heart was for them to be healthy adults, and that there was no scarier thought than imagining them at age 45 still acting like children and living in my house. Yikes! So how was I going to define it? When was the beginning of "adulthood" going to be? How was I going to lead the transition?

There is a sort of randomness to 13. No trigger that happens and makes it a good time. No magic beans or fairy dust to wave around. Just a date, and a commitment.

But here is the cool thing: I've seen it work. I've seen it work in ways as individual as my children are. My oldest son was embarrassed. He didn't want to be center stage, and he was ashamed that his parents were acting "weird", unlike all the other parents. He hid his blessing book in the closet for several years afterward. But the seed had been planted. He eventually embraced the blessings, and has carried them into his marriage with strength of character and commitment that are rare. He is a man, and ready to carry forth.

My oldest daughter was different. She cherished her blessing book, and carried it with her in her overseas travels. She turned to it for comfort and strength in those quiet and fearful times when she needed the reminders of who she was, and what mattered.

My second son virtually led me. He had seen his older siblings' blessings, and there was nothing he wanted more than to arrive at the moment where he was a "man". He studied for a year, and displayed an expanding desire for growth. I was a bit dubious - he was clearly not ready. He was childish in his ways, and had a lot of growing up to do. But the amazing thing to me was what happened *after* his Blessing. It was like we had flipped a switch - he was suddenly a man. He completely changed his attitudes, and suddenly began to behave more responsibly and mature.

My third son was also challenging. Rapid hormonal changes had left him sullen and disconnected - perhaps even a little "dark". Yet the blessing service again flipped the switch, and he came out of his shell almost overnight. His joy returned, and he is learning how to incorporate his blessings into the compassionate and thoughtful man that he is.

Each of them changed dramatically, and it was clearly directly related to the blessing service, and to our family and community celebrating the passage, and sealing the deal.

Blessing

THE NEXT
GENERATION

4

A Call to Mothers

NOTHING AND NOBODY TUGS AT a momma's heart like her child! And the bitter-sweetness of this event even for the mother is that it is a time of cutting the apron strings. After all, we *are* celebrating their transition to adulthood.

My personal experience is that our children's blessing services were a great time to express all that was in my heart in a way that would continue to edify and bless them as they continued to mature. My husband and I each wrote out separate blessings for our children. During the time I prepared each one, I asked God to show me something unique in each child; something they could develop as they grew. And then I waited and watched, expectantly.

It was an amazing experience to look at each of them through His eyes. As I would read Scripture, I would often come across a passage that just leapt out at me with relevance. I started jotting down those Scriptures, taking notes: remembering stories, making observations, noting dreams, connecting the dots.... Current situations, characteristics and behaviors assumed a new place in the plan and purpose God was revealing.

Just beautiful.

And so I call out to you mothers reading this: take this time, if you haven't already, to study your child. Look at the beautiful creature God has blessed you with – to raise and nurture and gently guide along the journey of her life. It is indeed a blessing to be a part of that journey!

Our calling as mothers is to support our children while they are young, and then to "send them off" on their future with a solid grounding. To sometimes call it out of them; at other times to encourage them to dig deeper and discover it for themselves; to teach them to be open to hear and understand God's guidance; and to give them the willingness and desire to follow Him in earnest.

5

Setting the Stage

ALTHOUGH THE ACTUAL SERVICE HAS looked different for each of our five children, *preparing* for the actual Blessing service was similar.

- **Memorizing Scripture** – As part of our morning homeschool routine, we read the Bible. Some years we work through a book study, or a word study; most recently, we are reading through a year-long chronological schedule. Additionally, we read a chapter of Proverbs that corresponds to the date. Months before their service, we have him or her choose a section from both the Old Testament and New Testament that especially speaks to them. We want it to be more than a verse, but not something they will find cumbersome, and something which they can discuss in their own words. Their choices provide a great tool to start some deep and real discussions, and give a great glimpse into the hearts of our children. They know in advance that reciting these verses for our guests, and possibly sharing a bit of personal testimony, is part of the Service on "their day".

- **Preparing the guest list** - This also we work on together with the "blessee." Planning who will be here to encourage our children is no small matter. We take some time to think about the people who who have touched our children's lives, the different influencers who have poured into their hearts, significant teachers and "heart friends", and others who may inspire, encourage and speak blessing into their lives. We start this approximately 6 months in advance. With about 4 months' lead-time, I have each child pick out special paper of their choice on which to print out invitation letters. We also send a letter to family and friends who live far away, and whom we know will probably *not* attend, but have had a significant influence on or relationship with our son or daughter. **(See sample in Resources)** Usually we go to Office Depot and look at the styles of stationary-type paper and they choose their favorite. The focus here is on personalization without being pricey. This also has an effect on the next step, which is...

- **Preparing the Blessing Book** - Here is both an opportunity to be creative, and to be humbled beyond measure at God's mercy and...well, "just" His all-around goodness. I have just *LOVED* doing these books for our children! Along with the invitation letters we send out, I include a blank sheet of stationary, on which the recipient will write their own letter of blessing, *whether or not they can attend*. We also recognize that it is not necessarily important that the people writing these blessings are Christians, or even understand what a blessing is. They can still *speak blessing* into our children's lives. As they are returned, I begin to assemble them into a large scrapbook, which will also include any mementos of the day. I save room for pictures and a page for the guests to sign that day. Really, you can put anything in it that would recall the significance of the event – *be creative*!

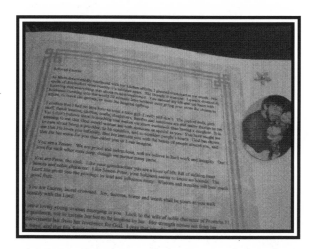

- **Creating the program** - This is something that is only limited by your own comfort level and/or creativity. If this is your first time, plan for and expect some moments of silence, especially if you are asking others to speak in public. If you *would* like someone to speak a blessing, comment or prayer aloud, make sure you ask them well ahead of the date. But to avoid awkward moments for everyone, and to ensure your family is all on the same page, it's also a good idea to review whatever program you put together with your spouse and kids in advance. Trust me on this.

6

The Day

IF YOU CHOOSE TO PLAN a special service for your child, the following sections may help you to plan a meaningful occasion.

Planning a memorable day starts with Chapter 5. Setting the Stage. This day with family and friends requires intentional preparation, so don't skimp on this part! And don't forget the food. You might want to consider including your child's favorite foods, or at least ask for their input.

- Chapter 7. Nuts and Bolts: A Sample Service outlines the actual ceremony, and I have included notes next to each section that explain and develop each part.

- Chapter 9. For Further Study provide some valuable books on the subject. Take some time to look through these. Most of them also have further links.

- Finally, in Chapter 10. Additional Resources, I've included sample blessings that we've written over the years. Please don't feel like you have to copy them in any way. I've only included them to display how different each is, and to inspire you a bit as you write your own.

Just as important, don't forget to read Chapter 8. Day-to-Day Blessings. As meaningful and significant a blessing service can be, over the years the Lord has impressed upon me how valuable and important it is to be diligent and pro-active in blessing our children out loud, and in that way helping bring out God's best in them.

7

Nuts and Bolts:
A Sample Service

- Open with prayer - father

- Introduction - mother

  I thank our guests for being here, and summarize some of the items discussed in this booklet: a little of why a Blessing Service was important to our family, a bit of history, and how we had prepared for this day, both as a family and individually.

- Scripture reading - child

  As discussed in Chapter 3: Setting the Stage, each of our children selected a passage of Scripture from both the Old and New Testaments and presented them to our guests.

- Pastoral blessing – pastor/elder

  We have usually been fortunate to have the friendship of our pastors over the years. Better yet, after our eldest son was married, his father-in-law, a minister, attended the service of, and prayed a blessing over, our youngest son!

- Presentation of gifts – mother/father

  We try to present our children with meaningful and/ or symbolic gifts. The most unique and my favorite was a bag of 5 smooth stones, symbolic of the power God had given young David to subdue Goliath, and a reminder of the power that even a young person can possess when He is standing and walking with the Lord.

- Blessing of friends and family

  Here we would read some of the more inspiring blessings sent from friends and family far away, and then invite some of our guests present to share theirs.

- Blessing of the father/anointing with oil – father

  A deeply moving time for everyone; and for our younger children we were able to use a bottle of anointing oil that Paul and I brought back from Israel a few years ago.

- Lord's Supper

  This is optional, but lends an extra-special feeling to the day.

- Final prayer and laying on of hands – ALL

- Let's celebrate!

Blessing
THE NEXT
GENERATION

8

Day-to-Day Blessings

THERE MAY BE SOME OF you who, even though you have gotten this far in this guide, may still feel a little out of your league, or uncomfortable with the thought of putting together a big celebration as described here.

That's ok!

But before you throw the baby out with the bath water, let me gently remind you that, as parents, we still have not only the right but also the privilege to pray for and bless our kiddos. With that said, there are other ways to speak blessings over them on more frequent ~ and less formal ~ occasions.

1) On a daily basis we can pray for our children by name during our quiet times. If there are particular issues that you are working through with them, find yourself a concordance, or use the online one here, and locate Scripture passages that speak to that struggle. Lift them up to the Father by name. He already knows, of course, but it's good for *us* to ask on their behalf.

2) You can then share that info with your kids, and let them know what you've done and are doing! Over a meal, tell them how and what you've prayed for them, or while you're sitting together in the family room at the end of the day. Follow through by asking them about those situations and how you can further pray for them. *Reassuring them in this way that their issues/problems/requests are*

important enough for YOU to pray about will most definitely bless them....

3) Decide for yourself the daily events that you'll choose to use as a blessing opportunity. For example, when they leave for school in the morning, before practice or rehearsal in the afternoon, at supper, before bedtime. Locate a Scripture that reflects your dreams and desires for them, or one that is relevant, replace their name in the appropriate sections and *speak it aloud* over them! (See the end of Sample Blessing #3 below for an example.) The first few times may be a little uncomfortable, but I **promise** you that if you persevere, not only will these times become precious to you both, but they will start to remind you if you forget.

Bonus Material – Blessing Cards

When I first started writing about blessing our children, I struggled to create something that parents could download and use to encourage them in their efforts. I had already written about our own blessing service in a guest post for another blog, and offered simple prayer cards, which readers could download and print out for themselves.

We were *amazed* at the reader response! They have since been updated, and I am so happy to be able to offer them to you as bonus material for purchasing this book.

To get your own copy, use this link:
http://patandcandy.com/PrayerCards4Kids

It will open the cards up in a Google Doc, where you can download and print out the entire set of 30 cards. Alternately, because they are in PDF form, you can send the digital file to a printer, who can then print them, cut them and laminate them for you.

Keep them in your purse, or put a set on the table or your night stand, and you will be gently reminded to pray for your children whenever!

Blessing
THE NEXT
GENERATION

9

For Further Study

ALL OF THE FOLLOWING MATERIALS will provide a deeper understanding of the blessing, Christian parenthood, and Biblical beliefs. In them you may find additional ways to further personalize your own blessing service, and perhaps even more so, the way you parent and live out your faith. Some of the following links are affiliate links, which mean if you purchase the materials using them, we make a small sales commission, at no additional cost to you. We graciously appreciate that blessing…and pray that you and your families are blessed by referring to them, as well.

- This is the original article I wrote, to which I referred above, appearing in To Love, Honor and Vacuum; the post I used to begin sharing about the wonderful gift to our family that is the blessing! http://bit.ly/2tPxu76

- Focus on the Family has a great series, written by John Trent, called Blessing Your Children. http://bit.ly/FOFBlessing

- Focus has also been proactive in encouraging families to adopt this tradition with their "Blessing Challenge". Each step of the way has tips, and they have lots of other resources to help you and your family create a unique blessing experience. *Come join us there!* http://www.theblessing.com/html/

- Jack Hayford's article in Charisma Magazine, "Speaking Blessings Upon Your Children", offers many practical ways of expressing simple day-to-day blessings, and a wonderful suggestion, with examples, to use the various compound names of the Lord (i.e Jehovah-Jireh) as personal blessings. http://bit.ly/HayfordBlessing

- A tagline for the website **Heart of Wisdom** is "Exploring Our Hebrew Roots", and this post called "Do You Bless Your Children?" is a great article for those who wish to further explore the roots of the Christian faith. http://bit.ly/HOWBlessing

- A book that we found most helpful for guiding our sons into adulthood was Raising A Modern-Day Knight, by Robert Lewis. Published by Focus on the Family, it is a wonderful book for parents who are interested in exploring the Biblical basis of the blessing.

- The very first book we found, and often referred to others "way back when" is Imparting the Blessing to Your Children: Your Biblical Heritage, by William T. Ligon, Sr. Published in 1989, it is one of the earliest modern-day works on this topic with which we are familiar.

- Written by the Executive Pastor of Sherwood Baptist Church, Rite of Passage describes the ceremonies that Jim McBride and his wife crafted for their 4 children: each one as unique and individual as the child it was meant to encourage.

- This article from the Journal of Marriage and Family, offers a very interesting history of "Adolescence in Historical Perspective." http://bit.ly/JMFBlessing

- The Power of a Parent's Blessing: See Your Children Prosper and Fulfill Their Destinies in Christ – Craig Hill This book looks at seven "critical times of blessing" in your child's life, and outlines the "how" and "why" of implementing the blessing at each stage. Excellent resource!

- The Blessing: Giving the Gift of Unconditional Love and Acceptance – John Trent and Gary Smalley A best-selling classic from two notable contributors to the calling of Christian parenthood, recently revised and updated.

Blessing
THE NEXT
GENERATION

10

Additional Resources

AFTER WE COME UP WITH a list of important and special friends and family, I send this letter out about 2 ½ months in advance of our date. It's just about the right amount of time to get the blessings back in order to put the Blessing Book together!

Date

Dear Family and Friends of _____,

It's hard to believe, but our son will be turning 13 this year! It seems as if only yesterday we were bringing him home from the hospital....

We're writing because we would like to invite you to be a part of this milestone occasion. As you might know already, when our children turn 13, we celebrate the occasion with a party that has Biblical roots. In the Jewish tradition, at this time, a Bar Mitzvah acknowledges that the child is now a "son of the Covenant", granting him both the privileges and responsibilities of a man. He is "sent out" with special blessings from God's Word from those who love him.

This is where you come in! We are planning a simple ceremony for Matt in November, and are preparing a special book of blessing to give to him, commemorating the event. We're asking you who have been special and important to him as he has been growing up, to contribute to this book.

On the enclosed sheet, we would like you to write your own blessings for him. A blessing is simply what you hope and pray for him in his future. It can be as general or specific as you're comfortable with. You can include promises from Scripture, or your own dreams and vision for him. If you're artistic, you could include pictures or sketches. We hope that you will be willing to do this, and ask that you do so prayerfully and with intentionality. We are humbled and excited to see what God has in store for our son, and grateful that you have been a part of his life.

If you're interested in learning more about the blessing, there is a wonderful little book called Imparting the Blessing to Your Children, by William T. Ligon, Sr. If you can't get it at your local bookstore, let us know and we'll get you a copy. And, of course, please feel free to call us with any questions you have. **In order to bind the book in time, we need you to send these back as soon as possible, but no later than _____.** We're so looking forward to hearing from you!

May God continue to bless you and your family, and use you to bless those around you…

Much love,
Paul and Pat

P.S. *The date of the party is Saturday, November XX, 20XX, at 2pm. If you're receiving this letter, you're invited, so please mark the date on your calendar and RSVP to (my email address) or call me at (my cell phone). Thank you so much!*

Sample Blessing Letter #1

A Blessing

The Lord promises an abundance of blessings and wisdom on those who seek to obey Him. "Be strong and very courageous. Be careful to obey all the Law…do not turn from it…that you may be successful wherever you go…meditate on it day and night…that you will be prosperous and successful." (Joshua 1:7-9) First of all, we would pray that He would cause you first to seek Him in all things, and give you a heart that is tender towards the things that are important to Him. May you truly be a man of integrity, upright in your actions, thoughts and words. "Search me, O God, and know my heart; test me and know my anxious thoughts. See if there is any offensive way in me and lead me in the way everlasting." (Psalm 139:23-24) May you walk in peace and justice, seeking to further the cause of His Kingdom; both protecting and assisting those who are weak, unprotected, or defenseless. May you lead by example, serving those whom the Lord puts in your path with a heart full of gratitude and joy. May you never lack for what is necessary to live, but may your possessions never rule you, and may you come to know what the apostle Paul discovered: true contentment in the Lord's provision.

He has blessed you with a gift that was also given to a king. May you come to use it in the same way that David did: to give praise and honor to the God of creation. "Sing and make music in your heart to the Lord, always giving thanks to God the Father for everything." (Ephesians 5:19-20) May your heart never become puffed up or boastful, but be humble and eager to share with and bless others as you exercise that talent. May your life be characterized by sweet music and harmony, with an ability to live peacefully among the brethren and the world around you; an ability to smooth out arguments and disagreements between people; a sense of discernment and wisdom in your dealings with others in perhaps difficult or challenging situations. And when you come to the end of your life, may your family and friends and acquaintances say of you "He was a man who sought after God's own heart."

Our prayer would be "that your love may abound more and more in knowledge and depth of insight, so that you may discern what is best, and may be pure and blameless until the day of Christ, filled with the fruit of righteousness that comes thru Jesus Christ – to the glory and praise of God" (Phil 1:9-11). May you always "trust in the Lord with all your heart and lean not on your own understanding"; that you would acknowledge Him in all you do, so that He would make your future clear and straight. (Proverbs 3:5-6) (adapted)

And finally, may

"the Lord bless you and keep you;
the Lord make his face shine upon you and be
gracious to you;
the Lord turn his face toward you
and give you peace"
all the days of your life."

Sample Blessing Letter #2

It is nearly unbelievable to me that you are on the brink of manhood! Over the years it has been a joy and a privilege to help and watch you grow - each day has brought me new opportunities to be in awe of what God is doing in your life, and how He is shaping you to be more like Him....

Your name, meaning "Jehovah is (our) help", was, I believe, divinely inspired: both daddy and I received it simultaneously and independently from the Lord. I absolutely love that both Joshua and Caleb were the only 2 spies to return from their investigation of the land of Canaan with an encouraging report, showing total faith in God's word. And from a character sketch I found comes this description that, in faith, I believe applies to your own life: "this name is the key to his (Joshua's) life and work." His calling and character were "marked by a singleness of purpose, directness and decision...(as he) set an object before (him), and unswervingly followed it". (Edersheim, Bible Hist., iii. 103) May it be said of your life as well.

My prayer for you comes from the Book of Timothy. Paul had much wisdom to pass along to his young protégé, and I'm sure his encouraging words will also edify you. I pray that as you continue to grow that "the Lord will give you insight into all" that He reveals to you. (2 Timothy 2:7) May you always present yourself to God as "an approved worker who does not need to be ashamed and who correctly handles the word of truth". (v15) And as you stand on the solid foundation that is the Lord, may your life always be sealed with the inscription "The Lord knows those who are His" (v19); that you would always be an instrument "made holy and useful to the Master and prepared to do any good work" (v21). Pursue righteousness, faith, love and peace (v22), Joshua, as you continue to grow into manhood, avoid quarrels and arguments, and be strong enough to show kindness and gentleness as you instruct others (v23-25).

I pray that even as you have learned from the studies we have done in Proverbs about wisdom, you will continue to study and learn on your own, developing a discerning spirit that will cause you to be a strong leader, a Godly husband and father, and ultimately a man after God's own heart.

I am thrilled to be your mother. I am deeply blessed that God has seen fit to lend you to me for a season. I hope you know that as long as I am alive I will always be here for you - whether it be to lend a helping hand, a listening ear, a word of encouragement, or a reminder of Where and in Whom our hope lies.

Be blessed my son, and my brother in the Lord....

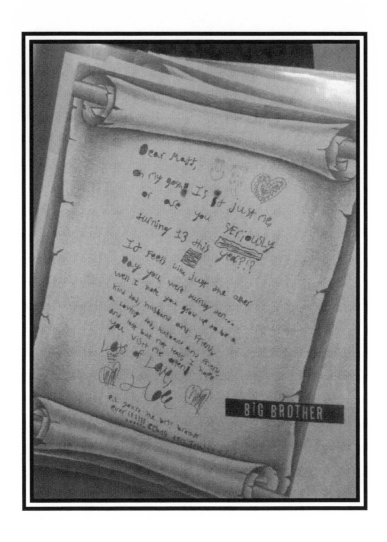

Sample Blessing Letter #3

I am so proud of you today. Watching you grow and become the young man who stands before me is one of the greatest blessings I have received in my life. It's been hard to put into words all that fills my heart today... A while back, while I was looking for something wise and wonderful to share with you, the Lord led me to this passage in Deuteronomy: "So be careful to do what the Lord your God has commanded you: do not turn aside to the right or to the left. Walk in all the ways that the Lord your God has commanded you, so that you may live and prosper and prolong your days in the land that you will possess." (Deuteronomy 5:32-33)

This verse is perfect for you! It starts with "be careful". Matt, you are a careful young man. Not only in that you have a caring heart and care about and for others, but you study much, also. In that way, you show that you are concerned about the work and the ideas that God puts before you. Don't forget to apply that also to your study of God's Word, for therein lies true wisdom! The passage continues: "do not turn aside to the right or to the left". The caution here is neither to be so consumed with study that you become legalistic, nor so lazy or ignorant that you forsake or ignore what He wants to reveal to you in His word. Your diligence will allow you to "walk in the way that the Lord your God has commanded", and by doing that live a long and prosperous life.

I feel so privileged to be your mom. I am happy to be a partner with you on your journey with the Lord, and in awe of the glimpses I see of the man you are growing into....

I have no advice to share, nor adequate blessings, other than what has already been provided by The

One who knows you best. Imagine my surprise when we were reading together just this week, and I came upon the perfect blessing for you!

I've paraphrased it here and will be praying this for you for years to come:

> *"For as the days of a tree,*
> *So will be your days;*
> *The Lord's chosen one will long enjoy*
> *the work of his hands.*
> *He will not toil in vain*
> *or raise children doomed to misfortune;*
> *for they will be a people blessed by the Lord,*
> *He and his descendants with him."*

Isaiah 65: 22-23

Blessing
THE NEXT
GENERATION

ABOUT THE AUTHOR

PAT FENNER LOVES TALKING AND writing about the topics closest to her heart: parenting and homeschooling. This book and another—**Celebrating the Feast: A Christian Guide to Passover**—evolved from family traditions she and her husband Paul have enjoyed in their 30+ years of marriage. Another e-book: **Homeschooling Outside the Box,** originally published by The Old Schoolhouse Magazine, describes some of the real-life activities she incorporated over the years in their own homeschool. She writes regularly at her blog PatAndCandy.com, where she shares parenting and homeschooling encouragement and tools and is a regular contributor to various other faith, parenting and homeschool blogs.

Blessing
THE NEXT
GENERATION